How to Draw a Dinosaur

Written by Judy Canfield
Illustrated by Terry Presnall

TM
sundance
A Haights Cross Communications Company

This is my dinosaur. I drew it.
It was easy.

I only used these five shapes.

You can draw a dinosaur, too.
Just follow my directions.

Get some paper, and some crayons,
paints, or markers.

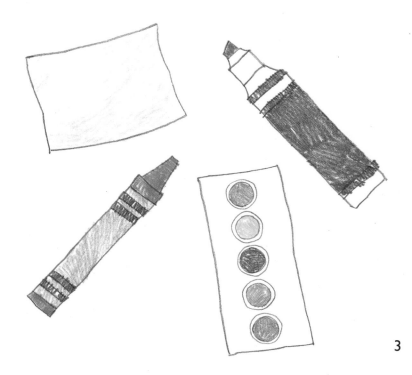

Start near the top of your paper.

Draw an oval for the head.

Draw a bigger oval below it
for the body.

On the body, draw another oval
for the upper leg.

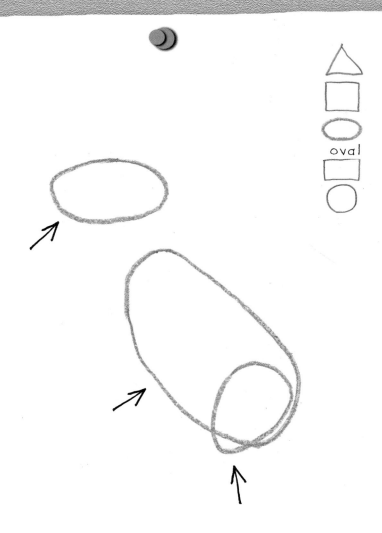

oval

Draw a triangle for the mouth.

Draw a square for the neck.

Draw a bent triangle
for the tail.

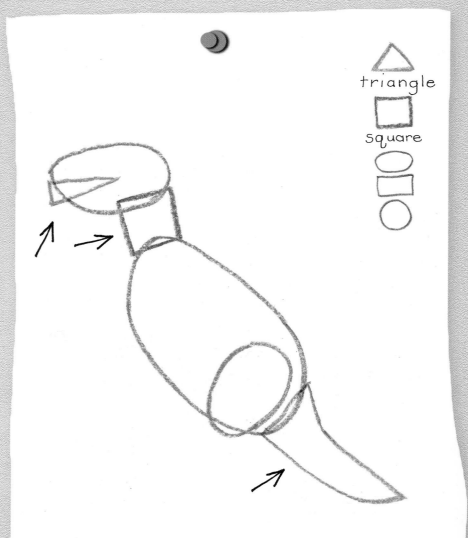

triangle

square

Draw two small rectangles
for the arms.

Add two bigger rectangles
for the legs.

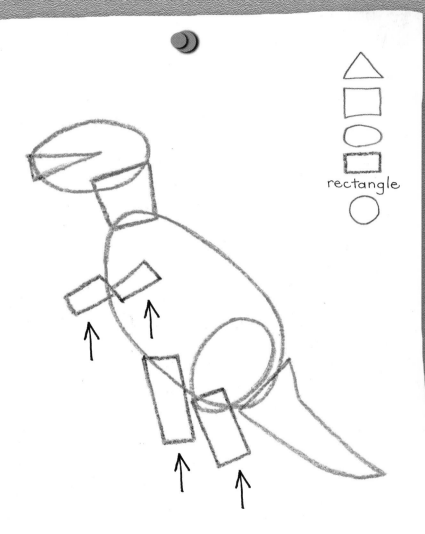

rectangle

Draw a circle with a dot
for the eye.

Draw a circle at the end
of each arm for the hands.

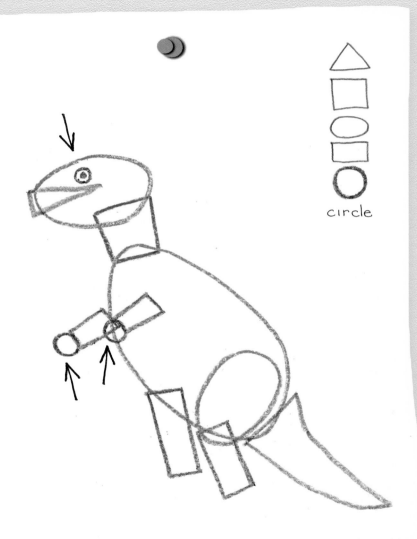

circle

11

Draw lots of triangles for the teeth.

Add triangles to make spikes down the back.

Use more triangles to make the feet and claws.

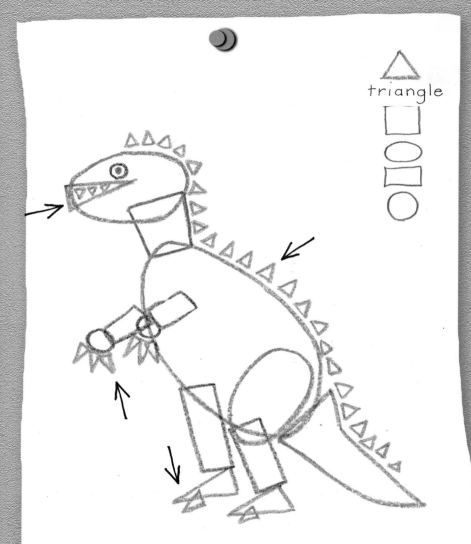

triangle

No one knows what color real dinosaurs were.

Use crayons, markers, or paints to color your dinosaur any way you want.

Draw land, plants, or other animals to make a background.

Now hang it up for everyone to see!

15